Nicki Minaj

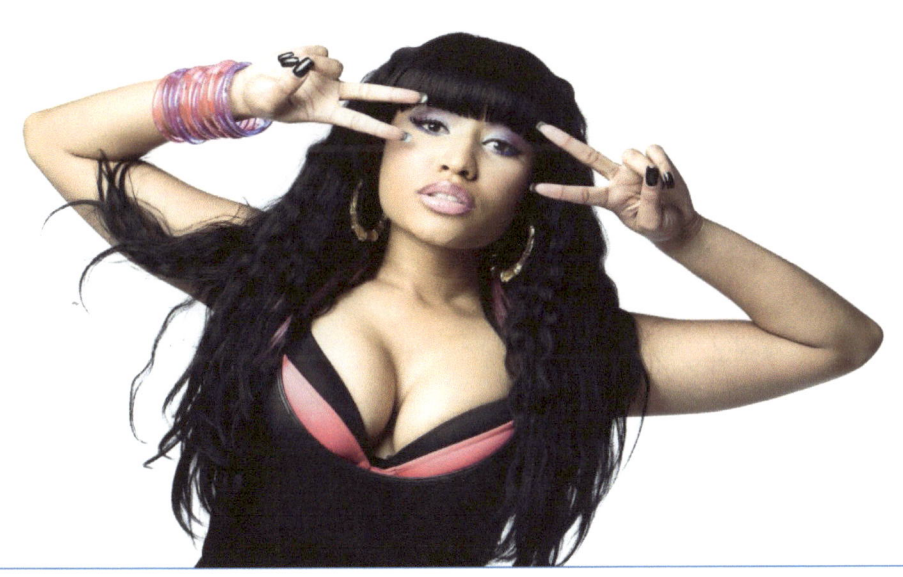

Nicki Minaj Photo booklet

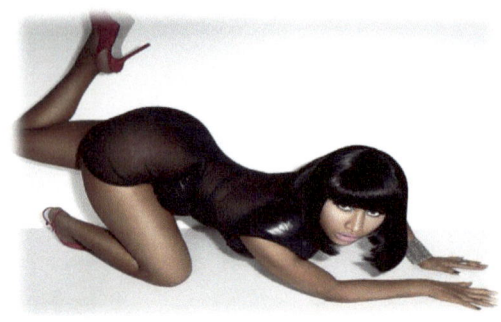

Onika Tanya Maraj , better known by her stage name Nicki Minaj, is an American rapper, singer, songwriter and actress. After success with three mixtapes released between 2007 and 2009, Minaj signed to Young Money.

Rapper/Singer Nicki Minaj (born Onika Tanya Maraj) has much more to offer than just a cute face, a sassy attitude, and a hot verse. With songs like "Your Love" and "Right Thru Me," Nicki has demonstrated an ability to craft songs that showcase her fierce rhyming skill in an honest and vulnerable way. Born in Trinidad, Nicki moved to Queens, New York with her family and made a buzz on underground mixtapes before signing to Lil Wayne's Young Money team in 2009. Her loud fashion sense, vocal versatility and animated performances make her as hip-hop as it gets. Nicki debuted at number 1 on the charts with her first LP, *Pink Friday,* in 2010 and followed with *Pink Friday: Roman Reloade*d in 2012. She is stamping her name on everything from fragrances and fashion to movies and acting (in the 2014 film *The Other Woman*). She was also a judge for the 12th season of *American Idol*.

For 2013, Nicki Minaj web worth is estimated at $4 5 million. She's lately become the very first female hip hop recording artist enlisted on MTV's Yearly Most Popular MCs graph. A number of her supporters have indicated this is the exact same as to declare that Minaj is the most powerful female rapper ever. But, the others often see this vocalist more critically and see the rationale she is even regarded as a star is her strange look, not her gift for music.

Nicki Minaj Photo booklet

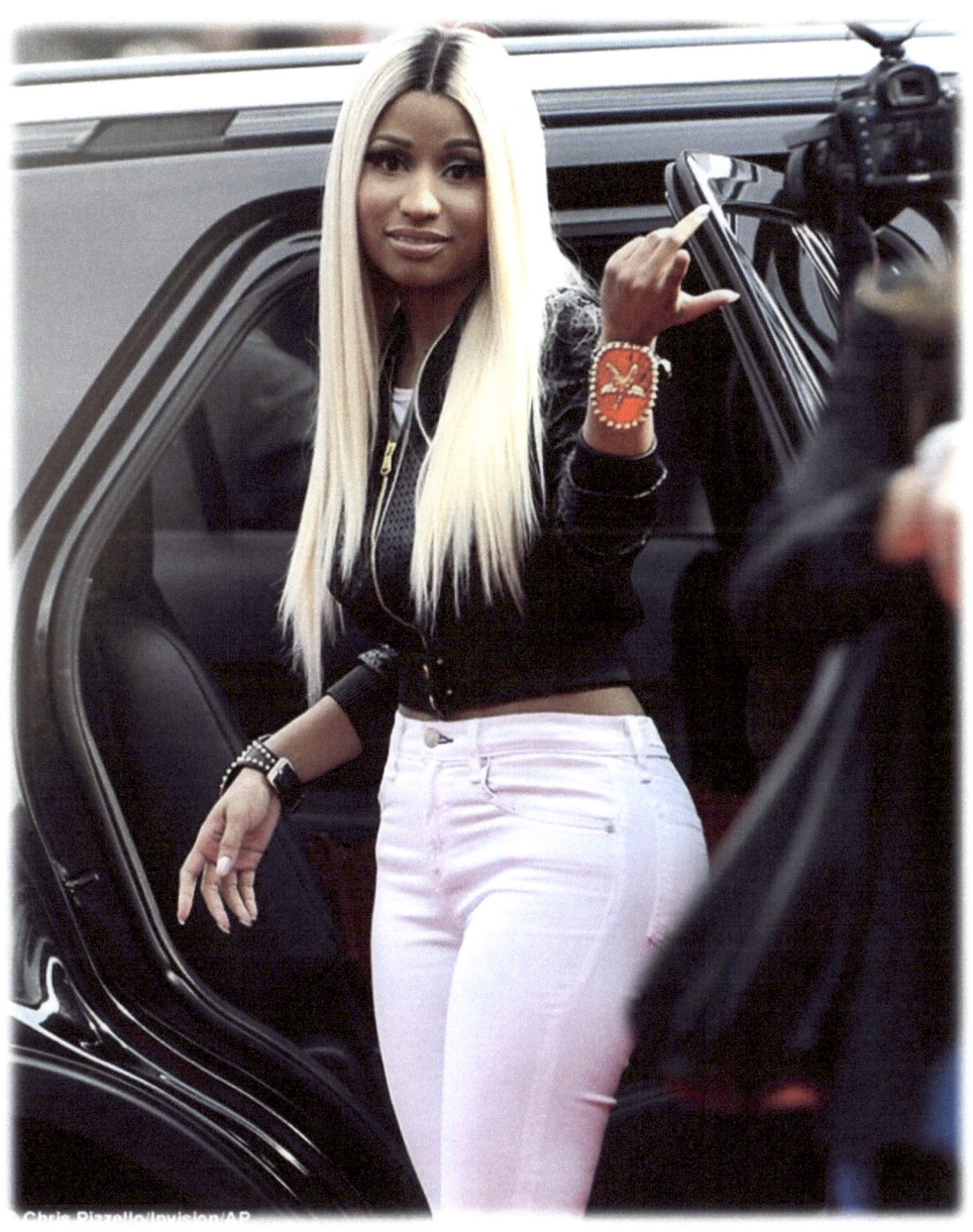

Nicki Minaj Photo booklet

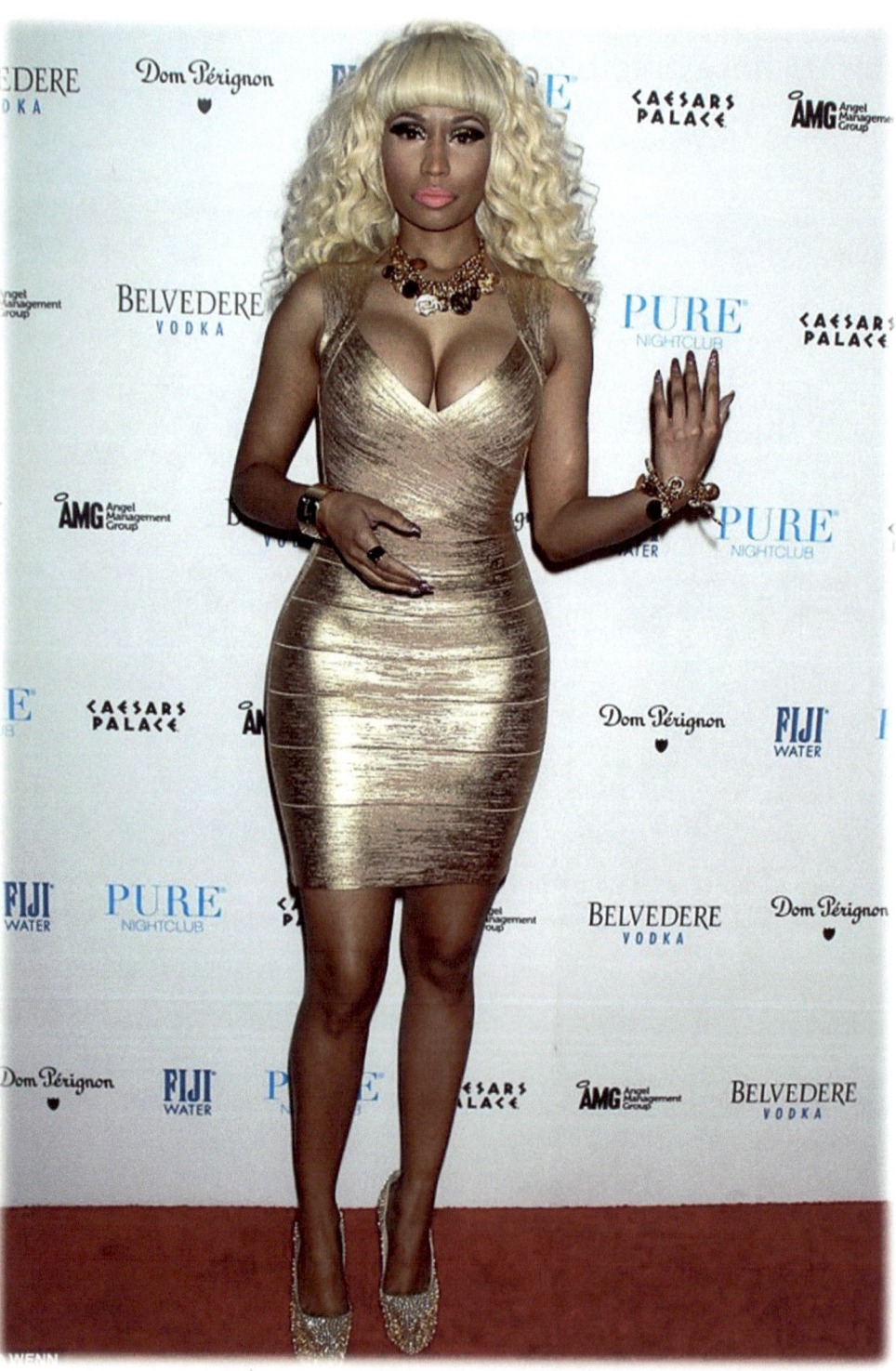

Nicki Minaj Photo booklet

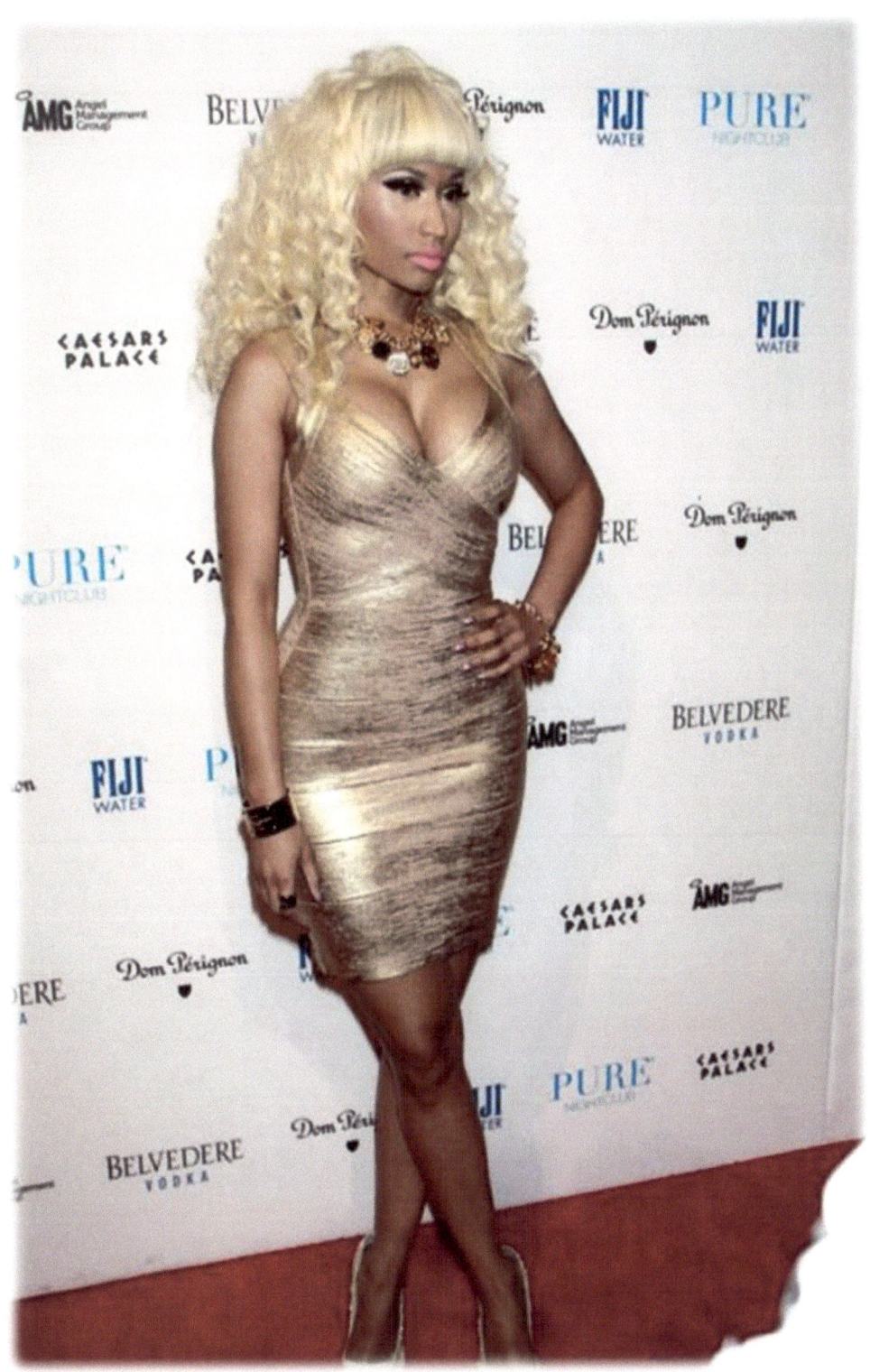

Nicki Minaj Photo booklet

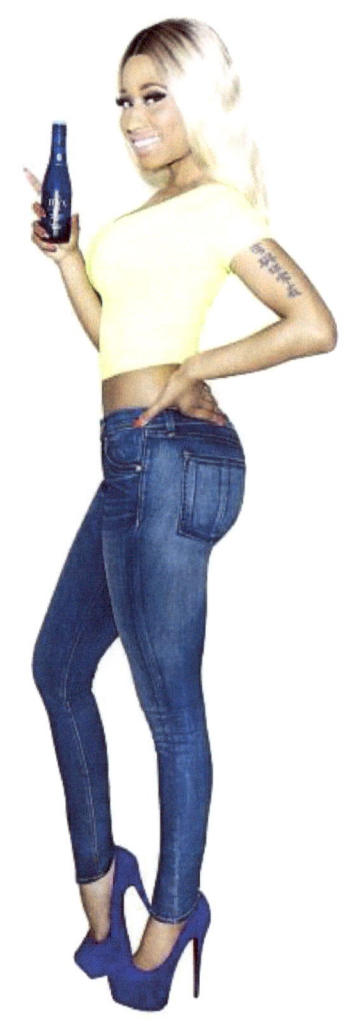

Nicki Minaj Photo booklet

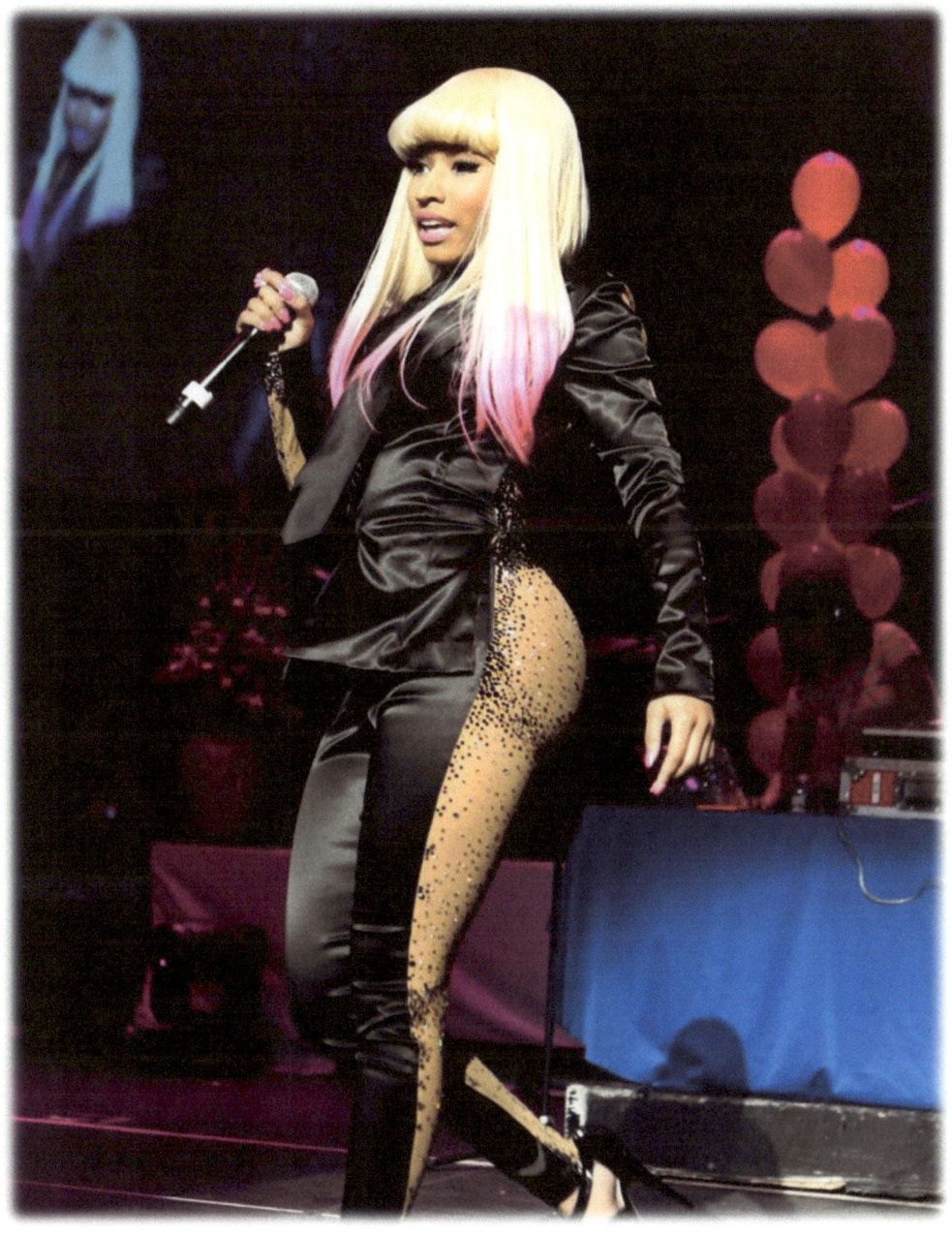

Nicki Minaj Photo booklet

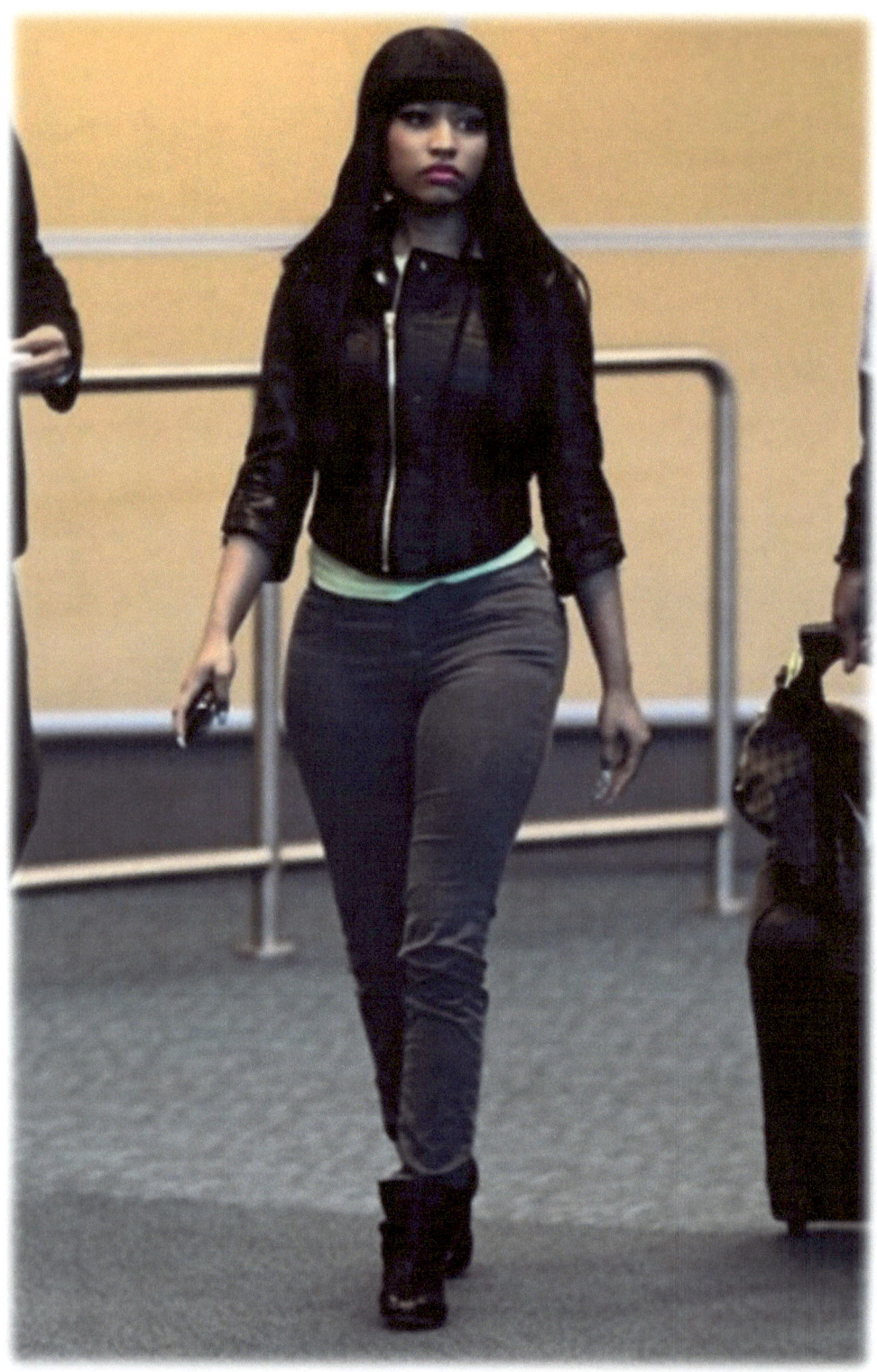

Nicki Minaj Photo booklet

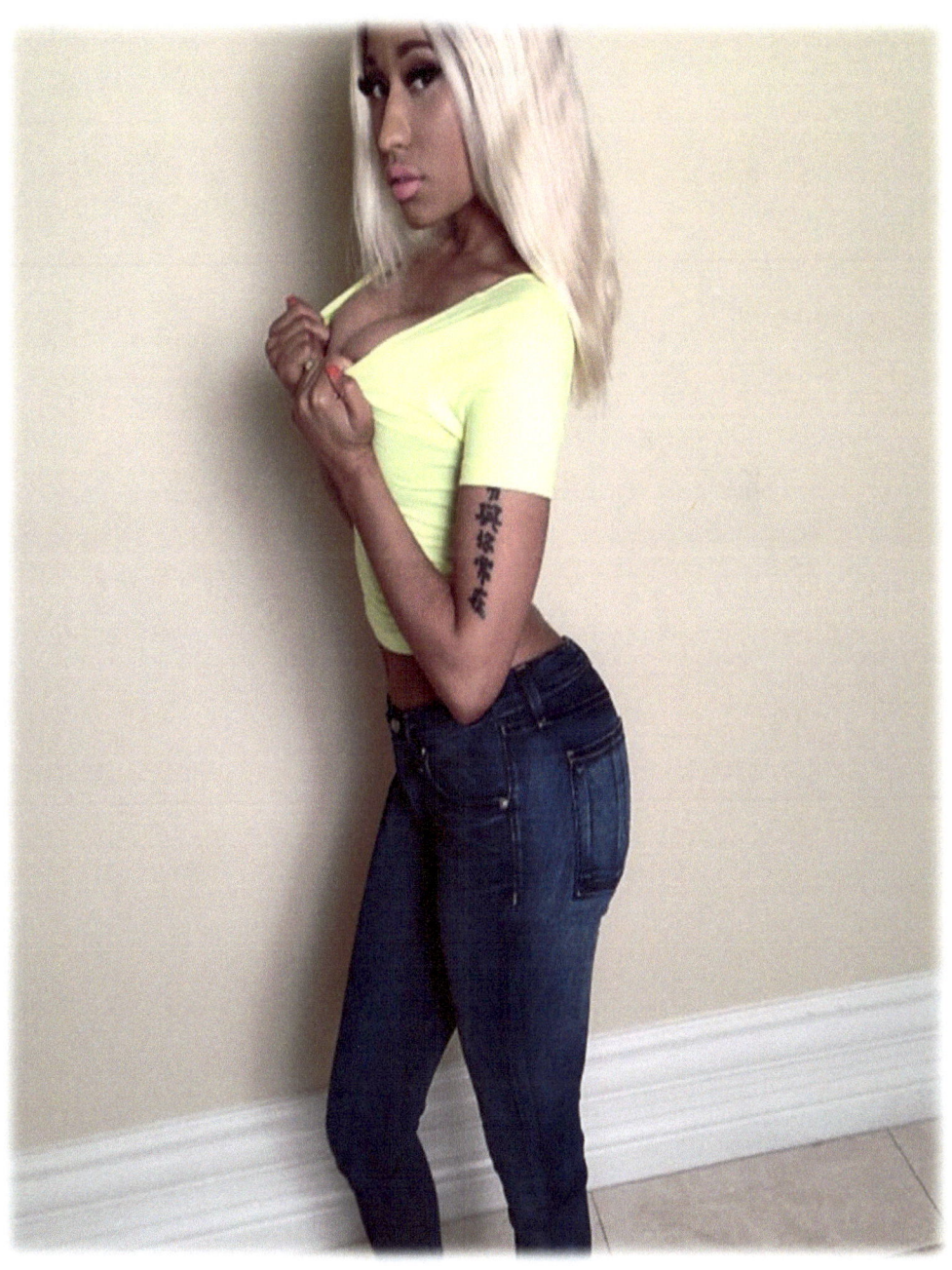

Nicki Minaj Photo booklet

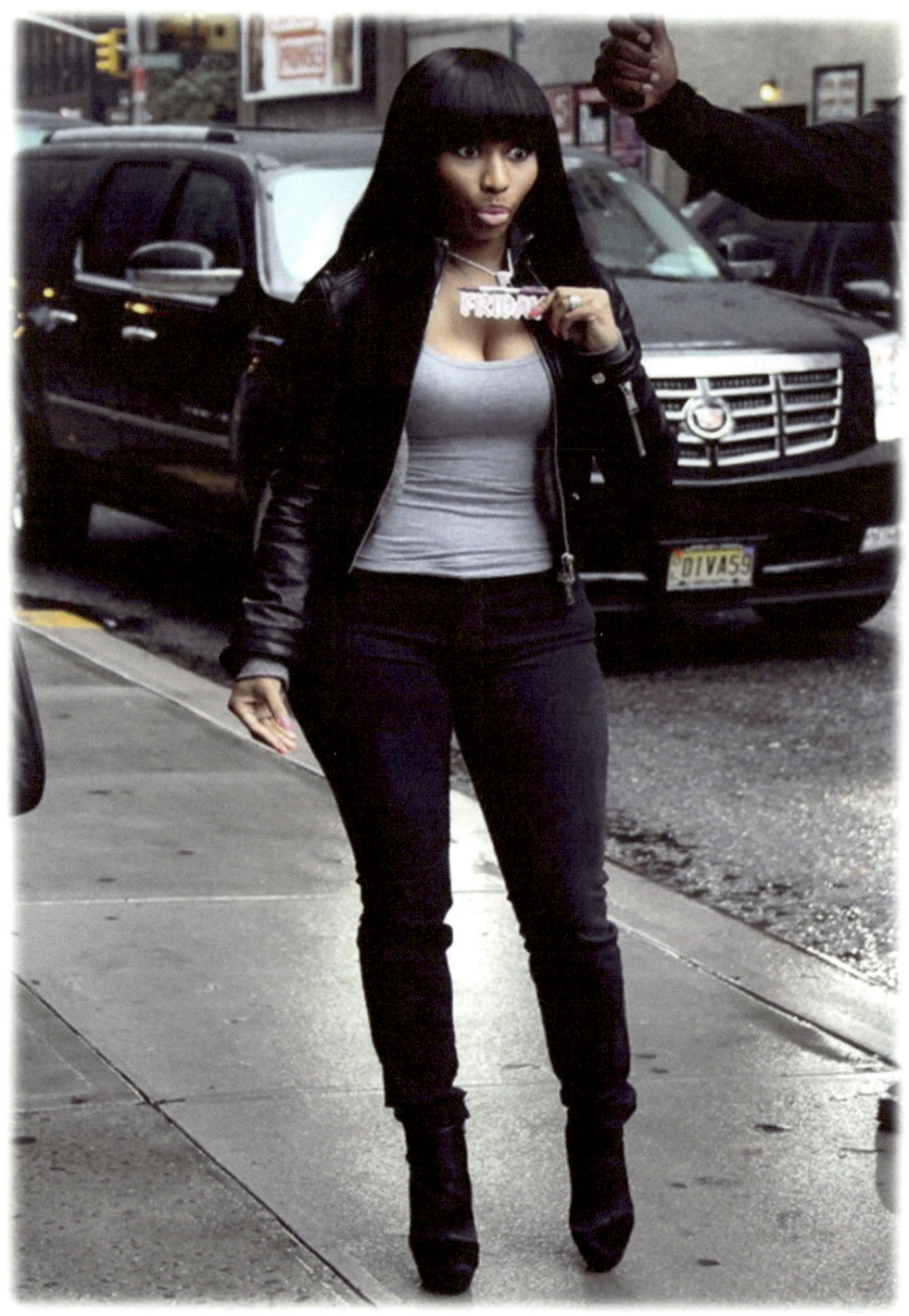

Nicki Minaj Photo booklet

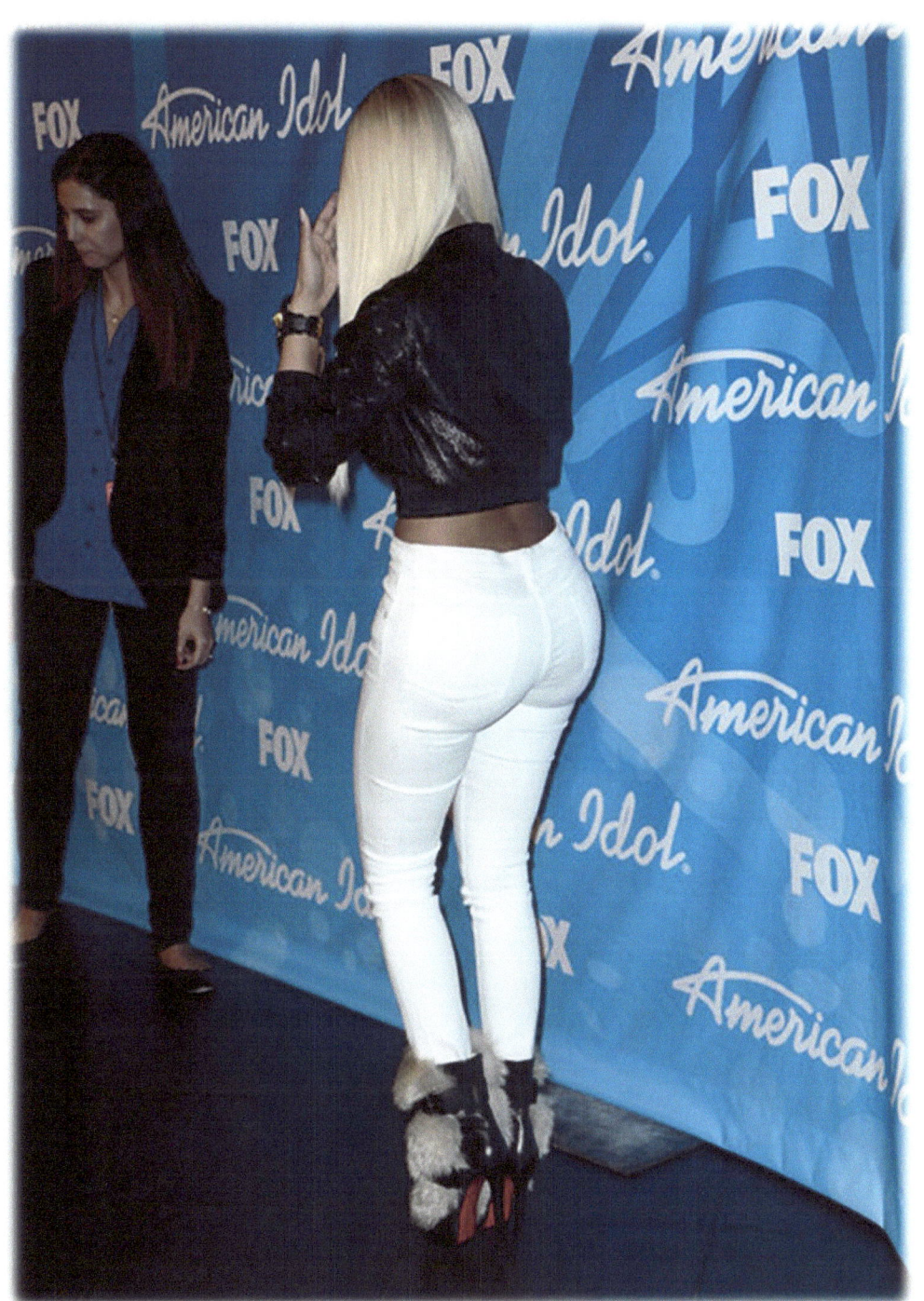

Nicki Minaj Photo booklet

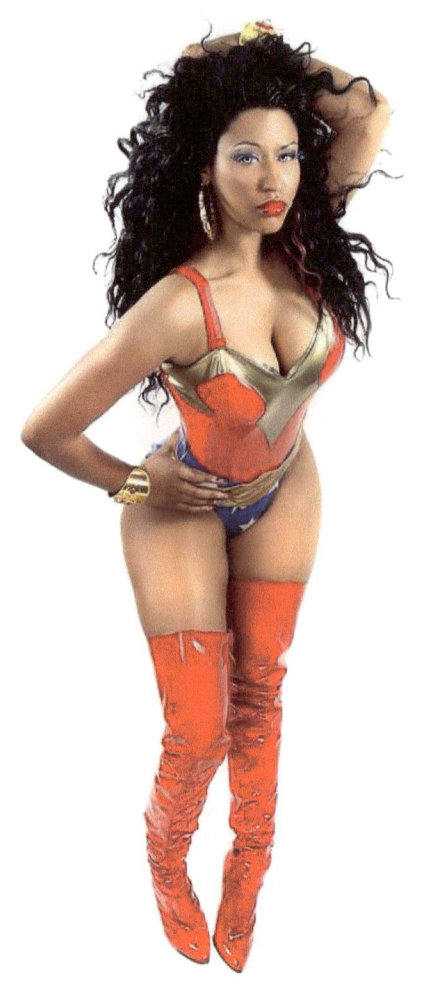

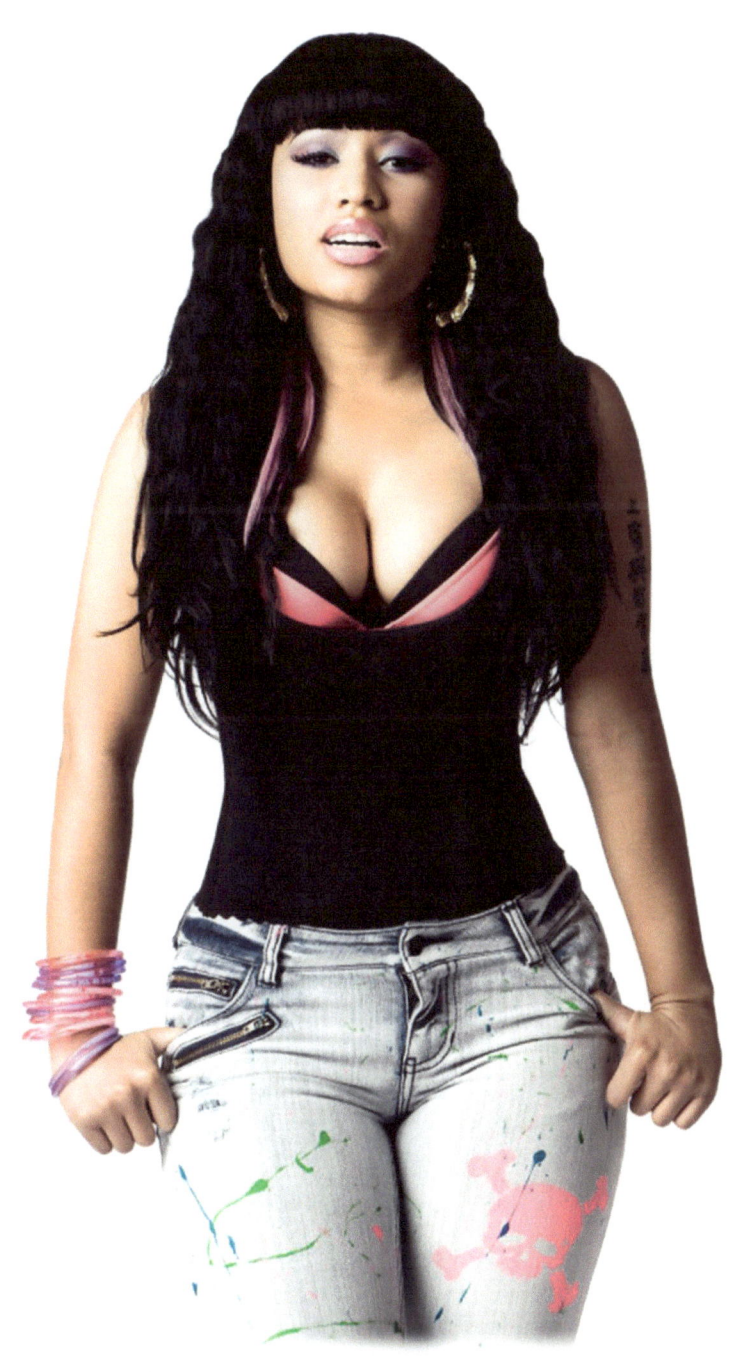

Nicki Minaj Photo booklet

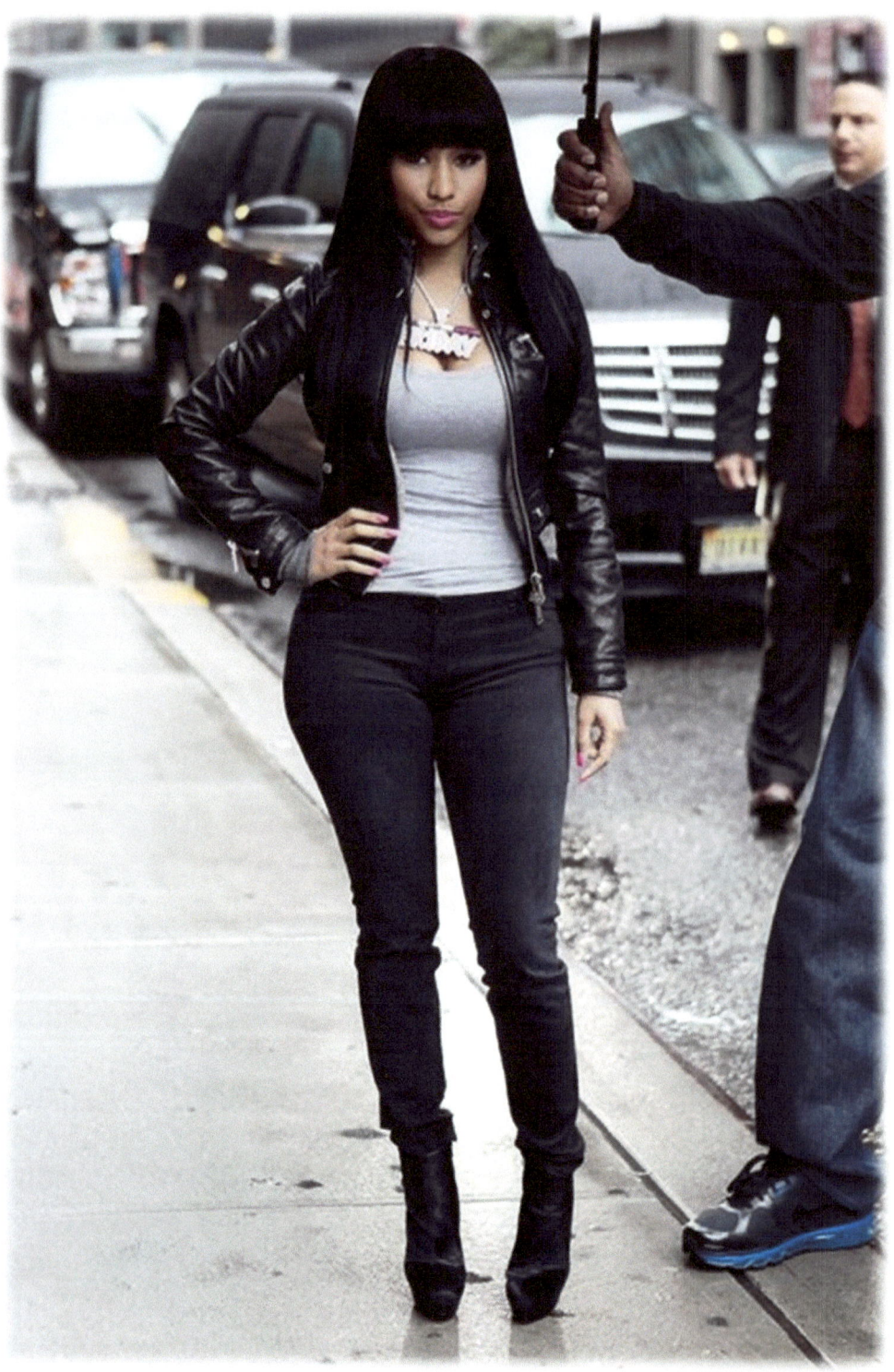

Nicki Minaj Photo booklet

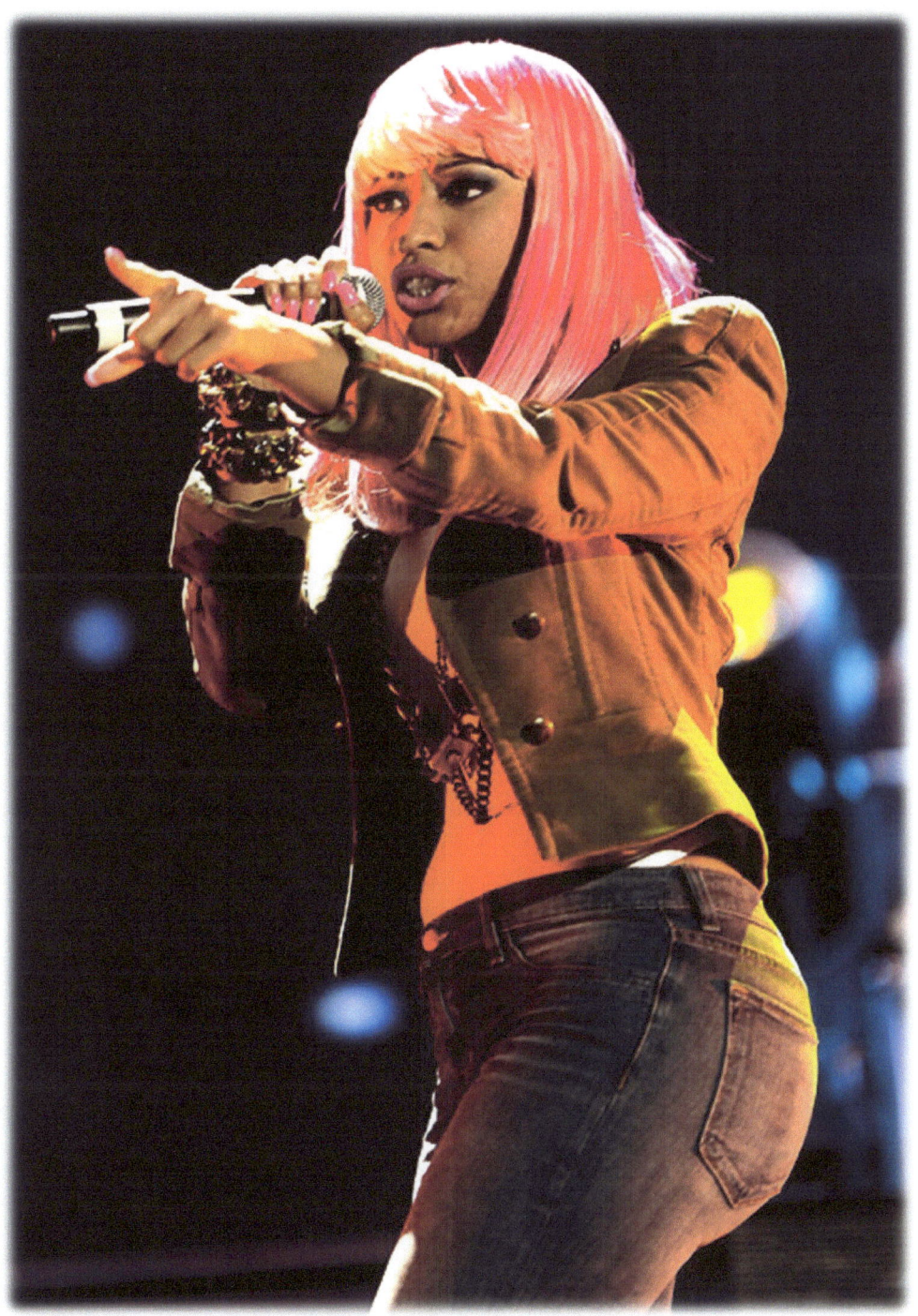

Nicki Minaj Photo booklet

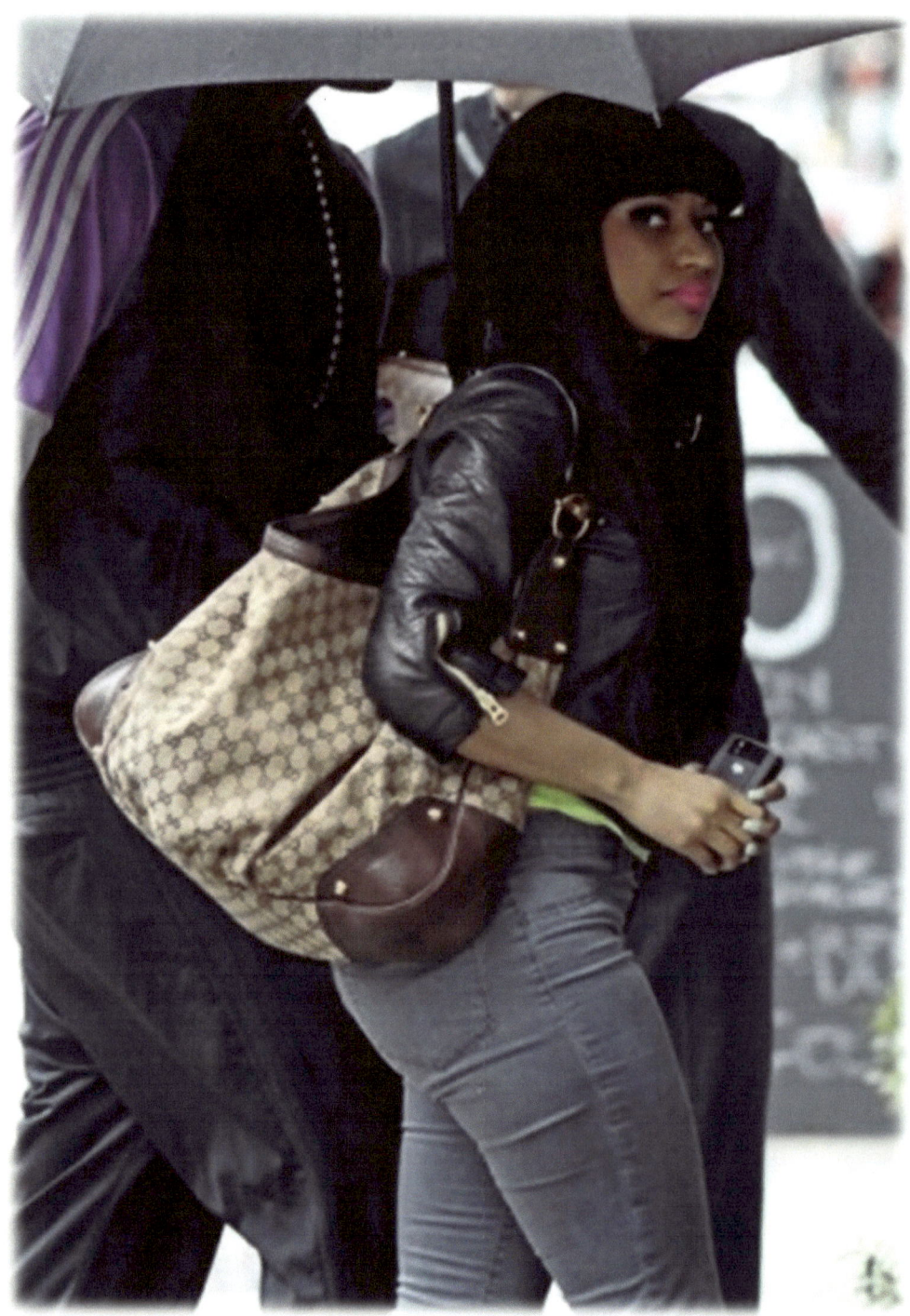

Nicki Minaj Photo booklet

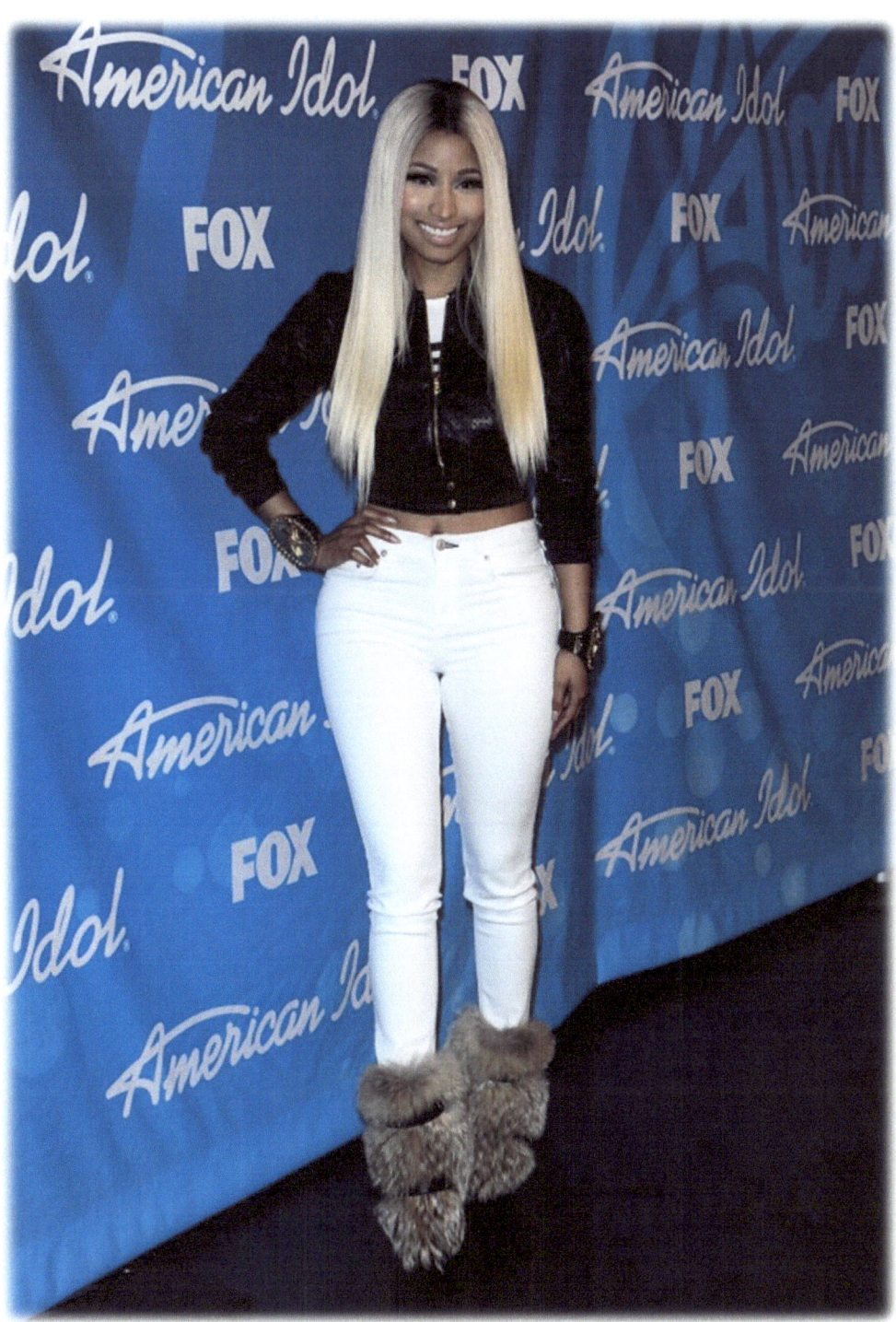

Nicki Minaj Photo booklet

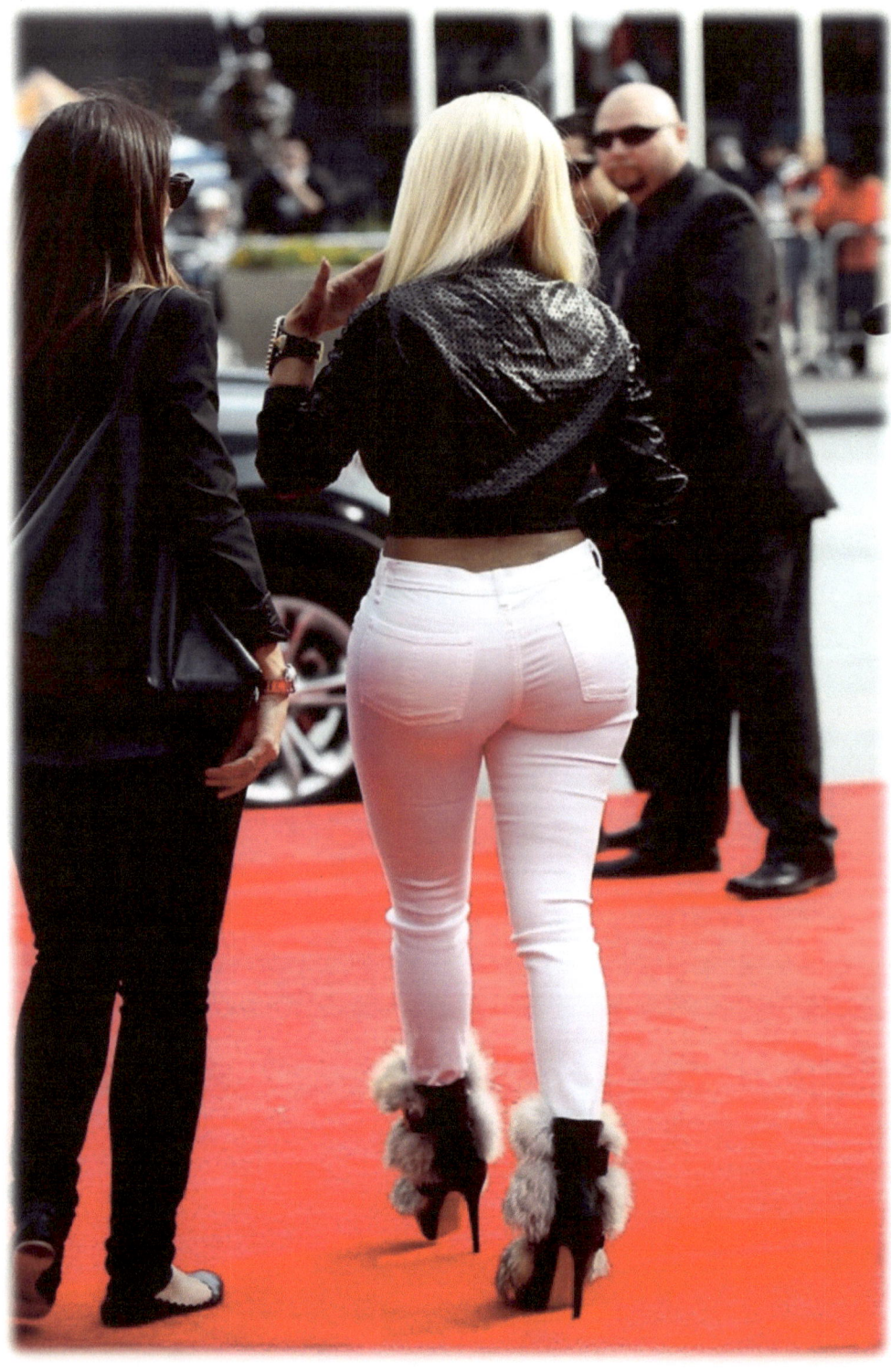

Nicki Minaj Photo booklet

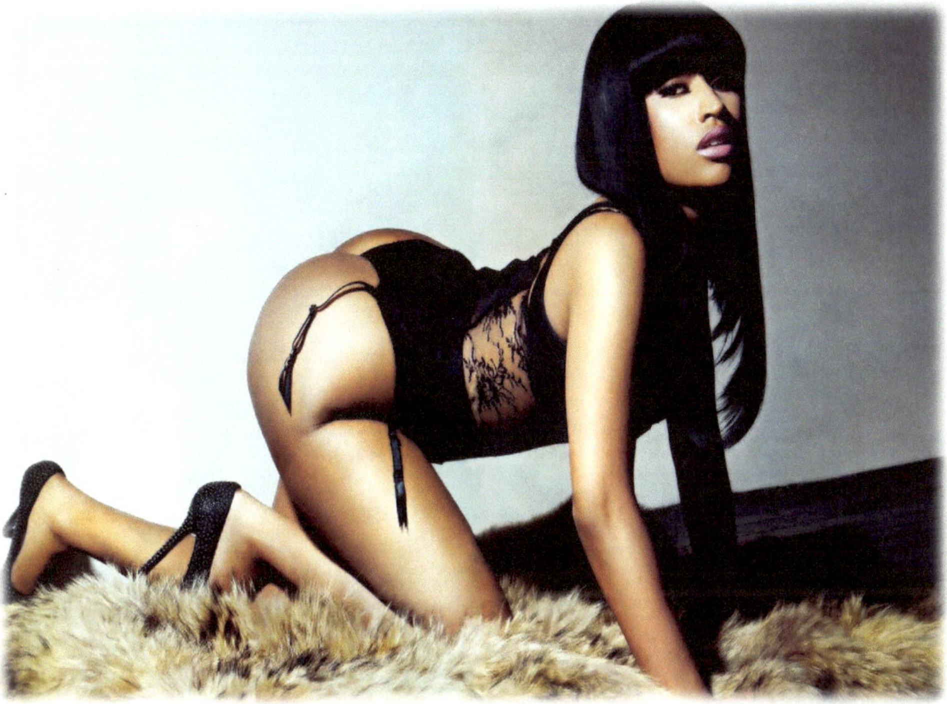

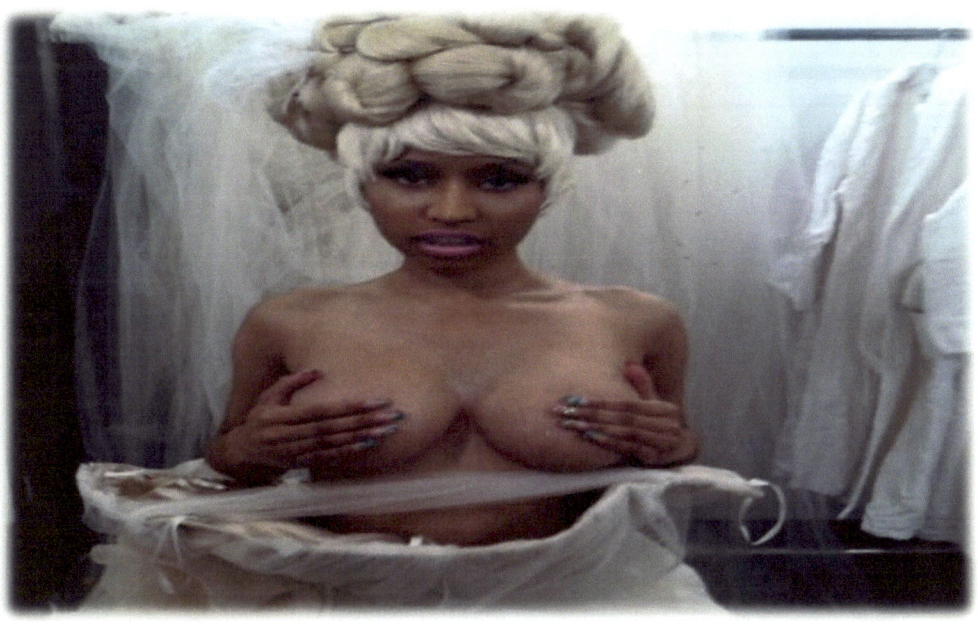

Nicki Minaj Photo booklet

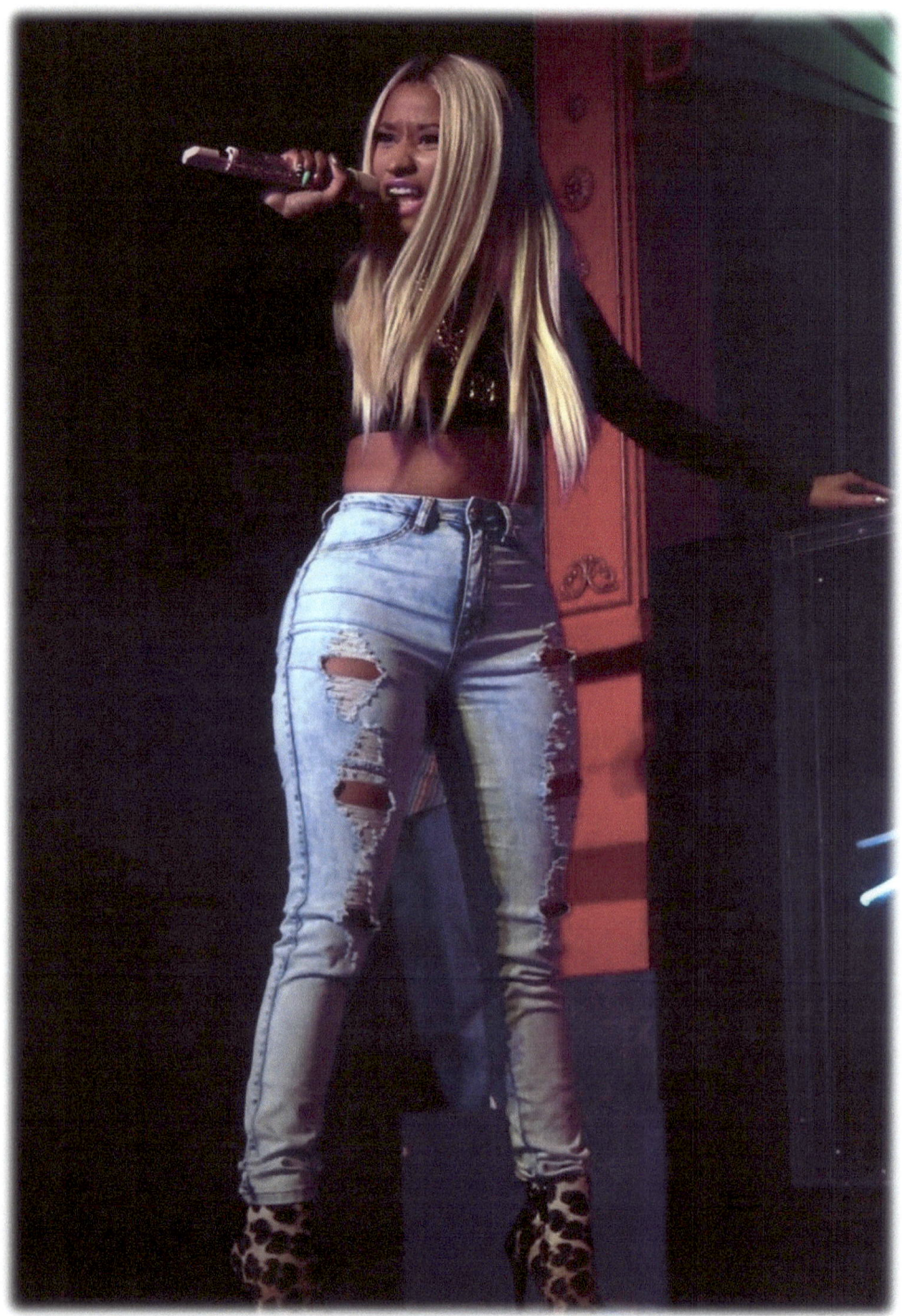

Nicki Minaj Photo booklet

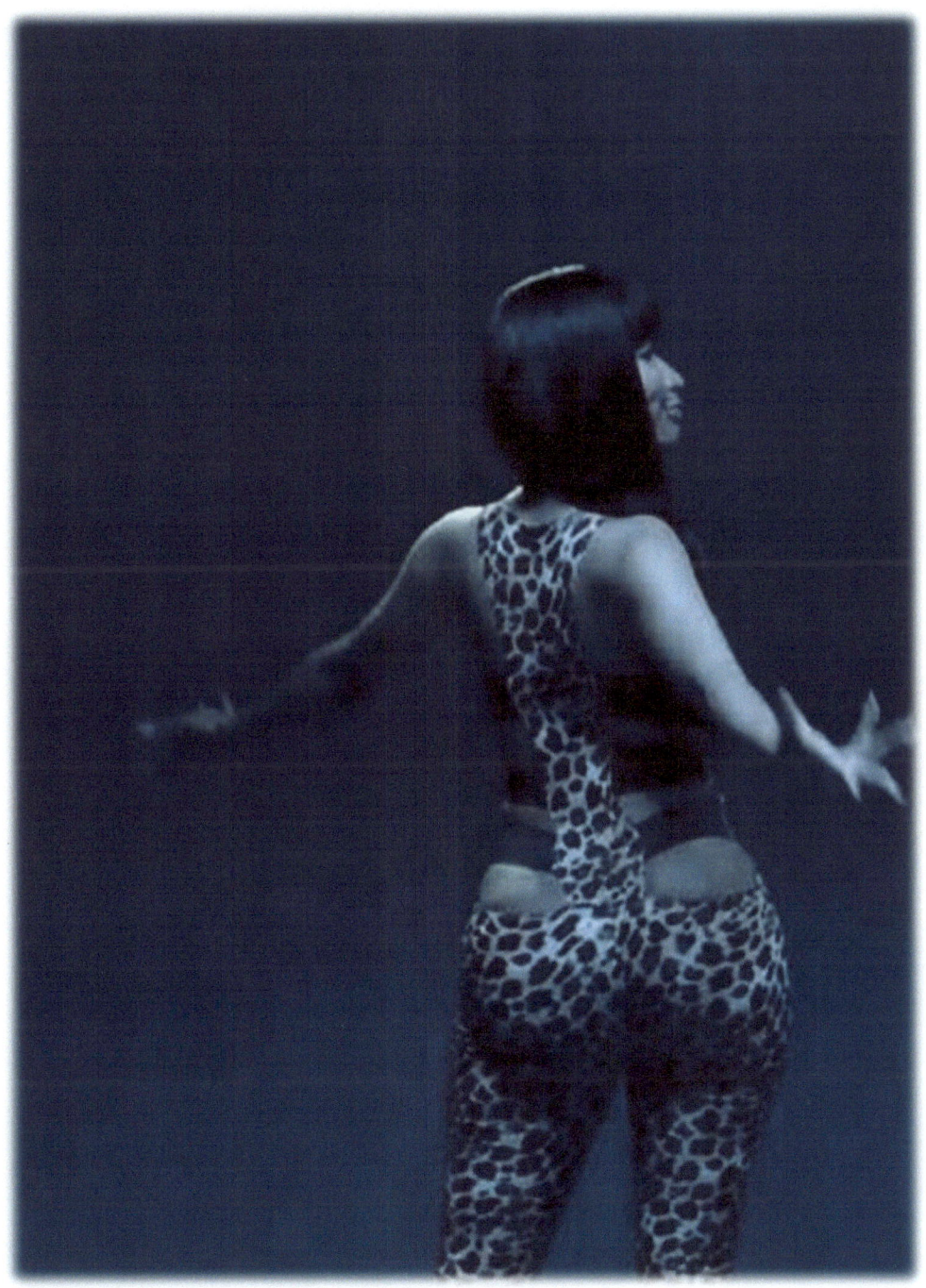

Nicki Minaj Photo booklet

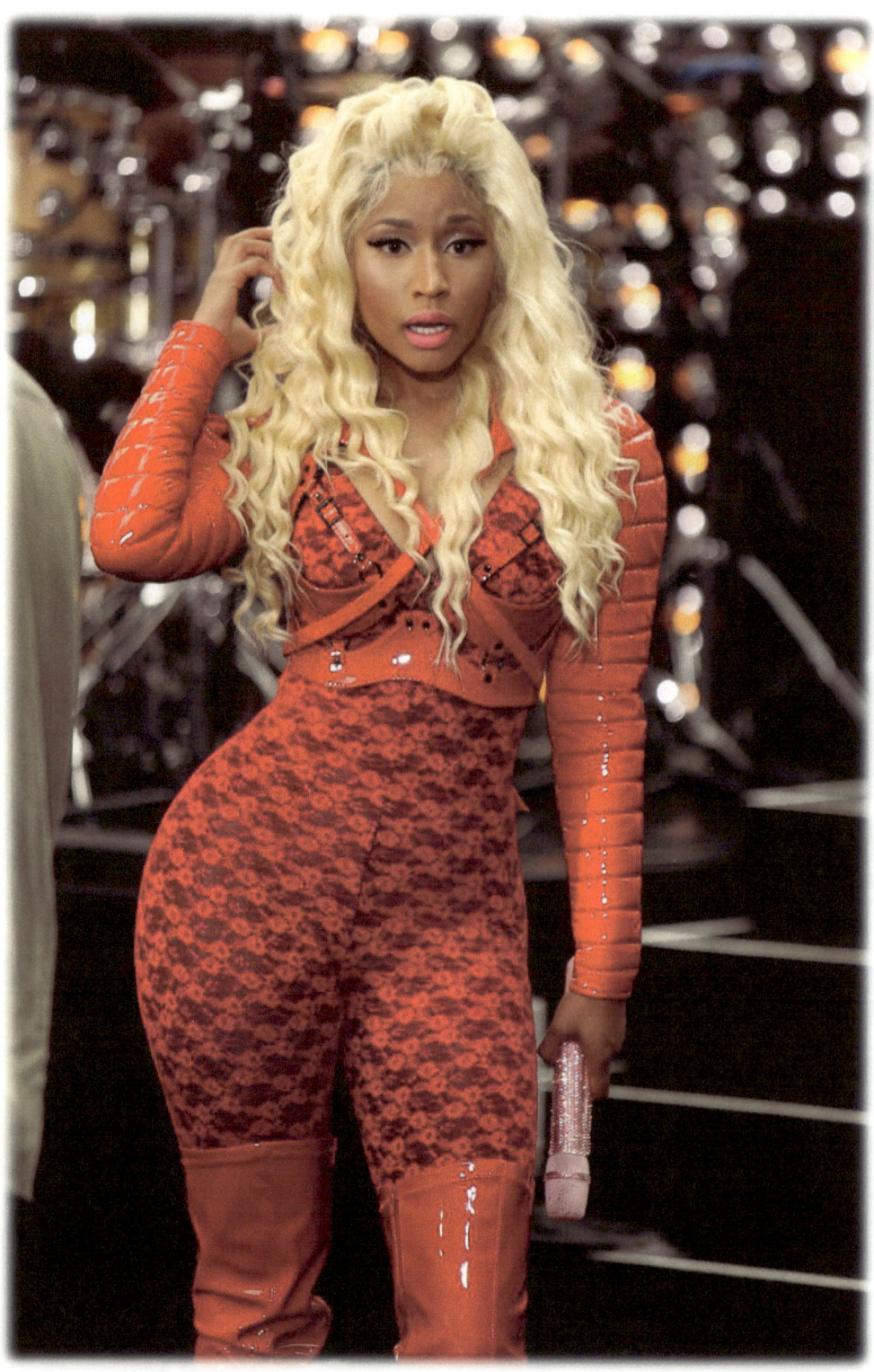

Nicki Minaj Photo booklet

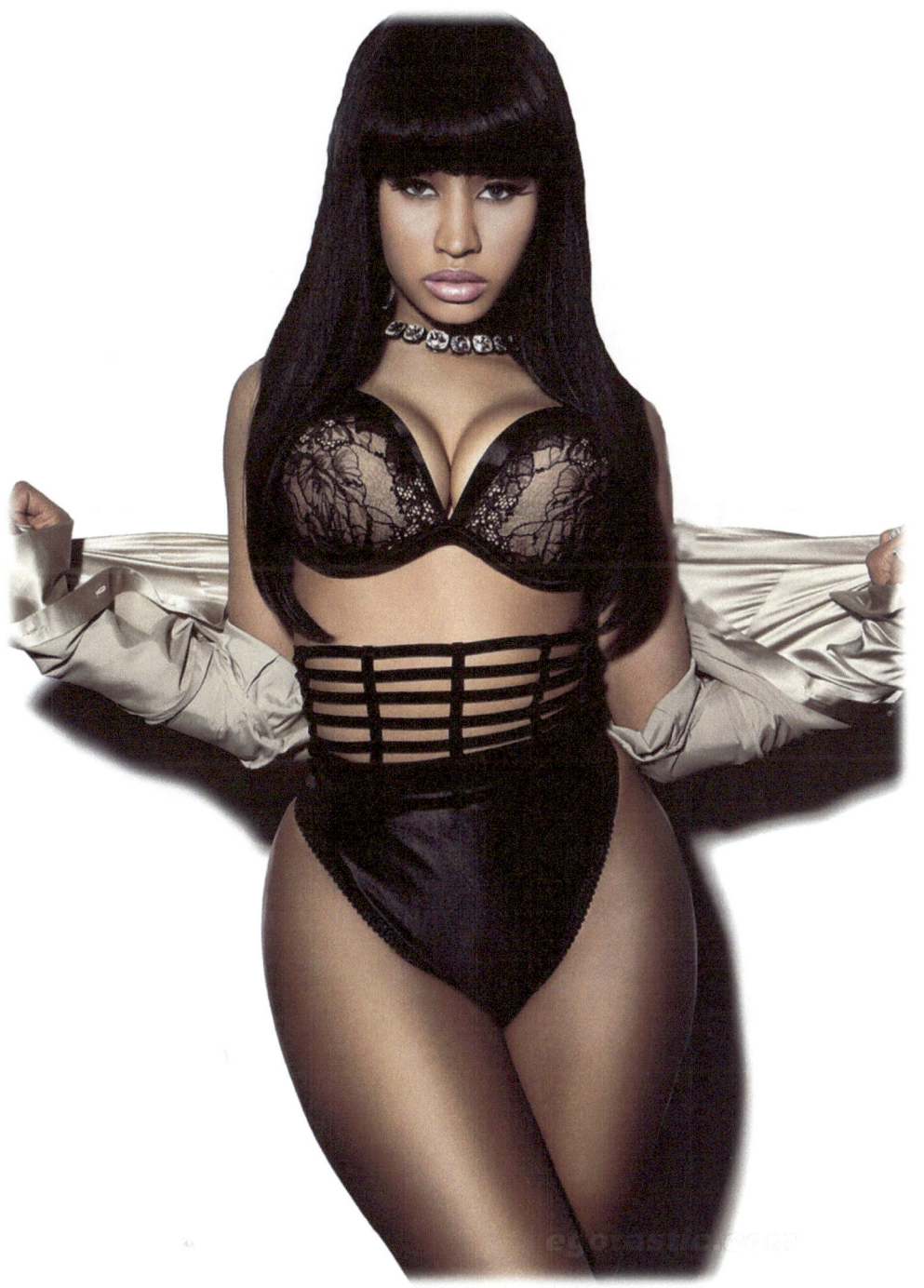

Nicki Minaj Photo booklet

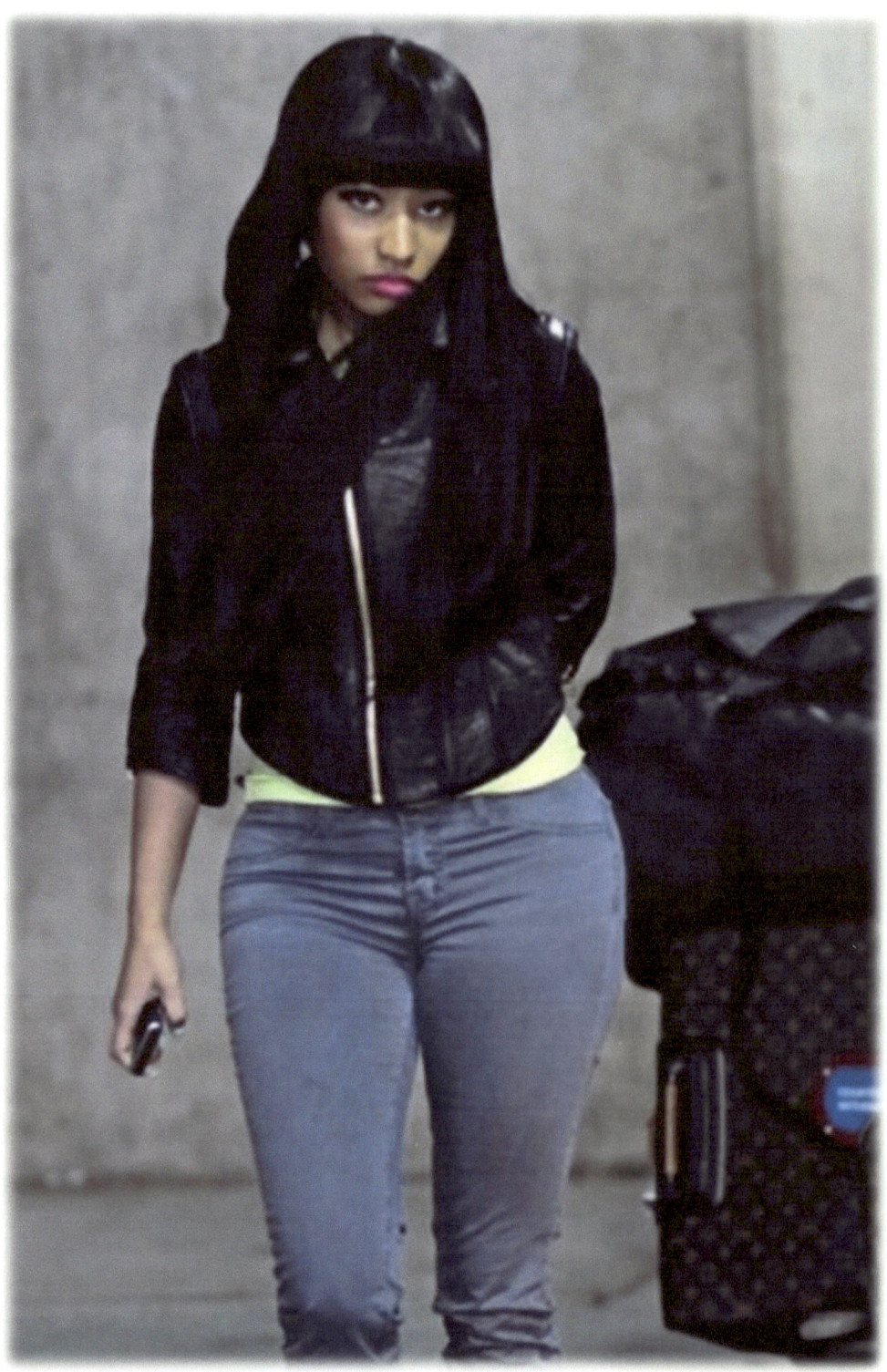

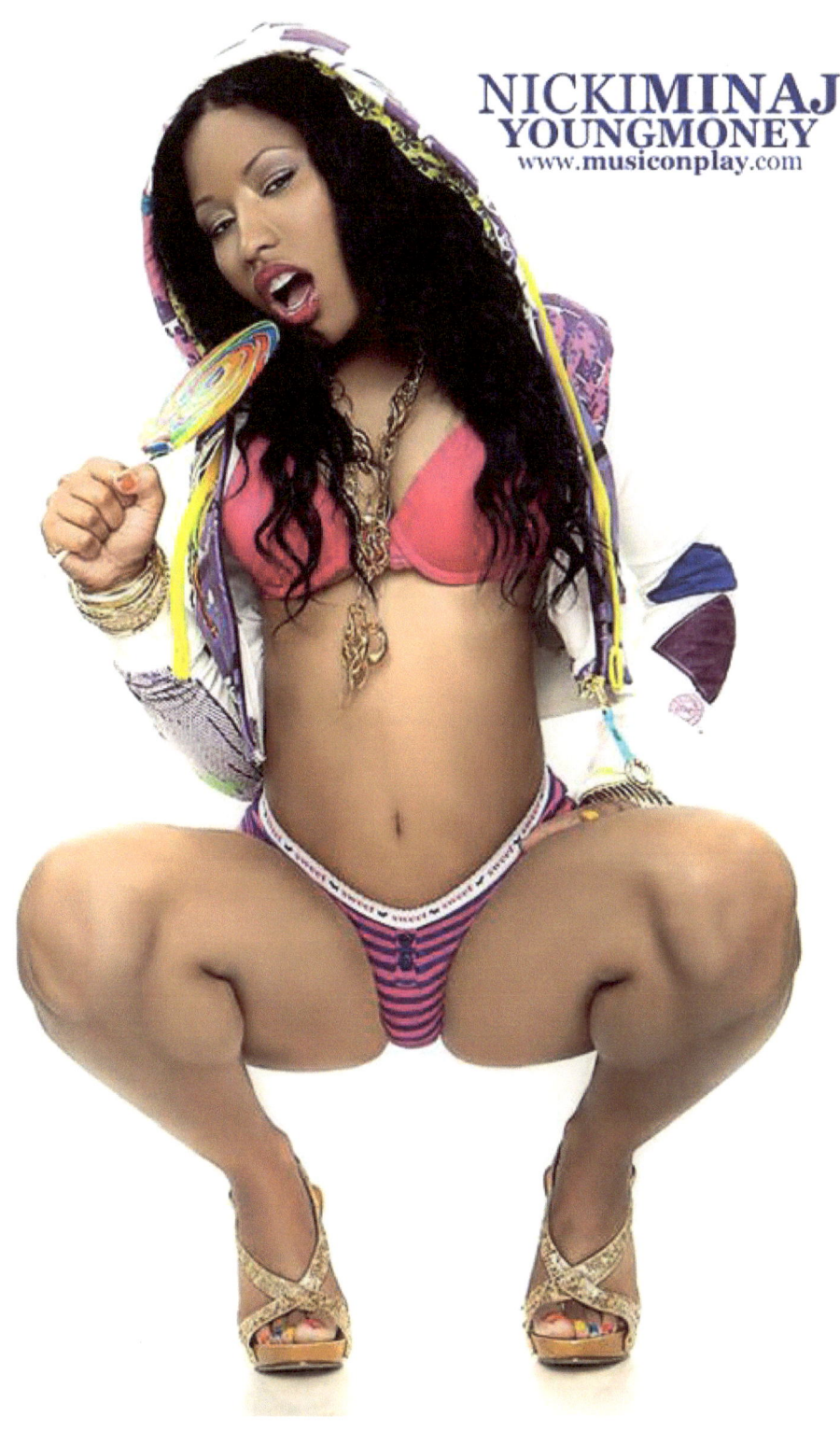

Nicki Minaj Photo booklet

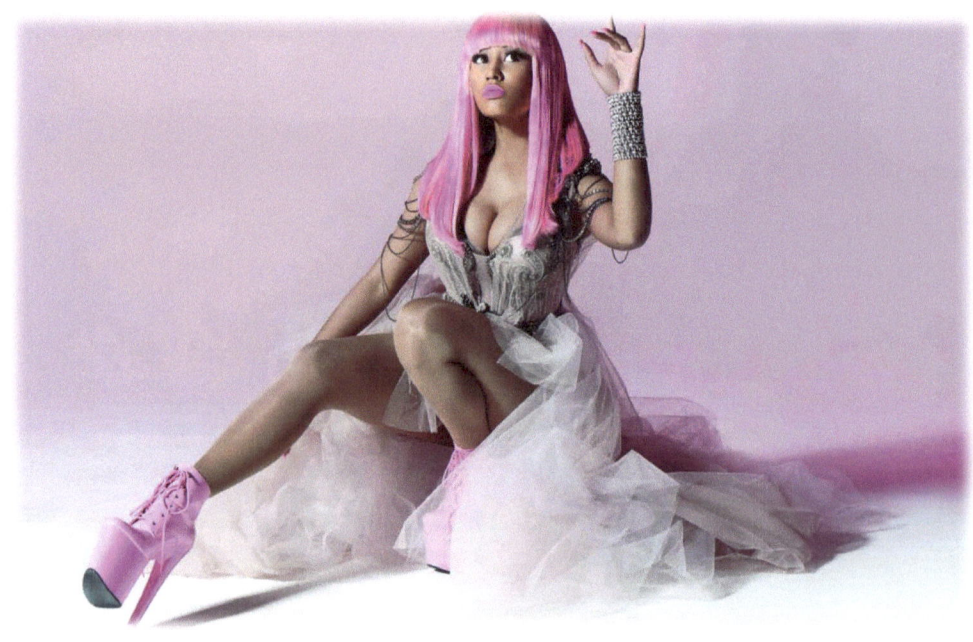

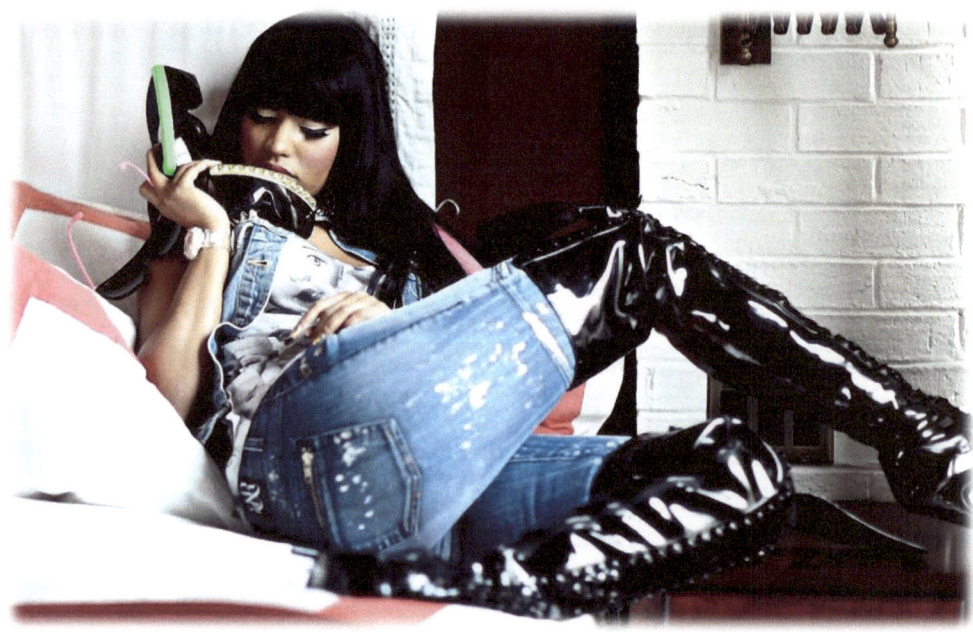

Nicki Minaj Photo booklet

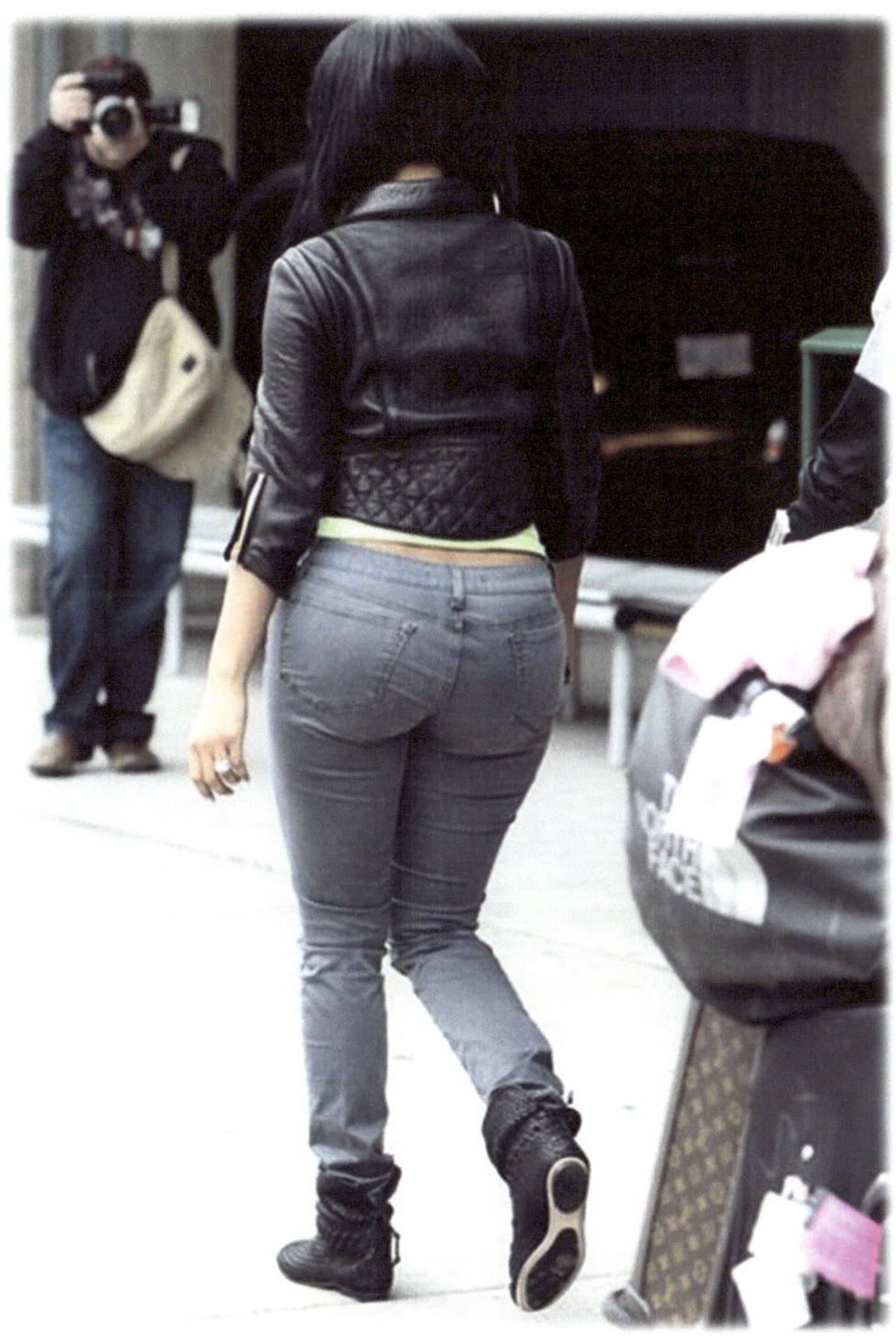